in the Institute
of Management

F O U N D A T I O N

The Institute of Management (IM) exists to promote
the development, exercise and recognition of
professional management. The Institute embraces
all levels of management from student to chief
executive and supports its own Foundation which
provides a unique portfolio of services for all
managers, enabling them to develop skills and
achieve management excellence.

For information on the various levels and benefits of
membership, please contact:

Department HS
Institute of Management
Cottingham Road
Corby
Northants NN17 1TT

Tel: 01536 204222
Fax: 01536 201651

This series is commissioned by the Institute of
Management Foundation.

C O N T E N T S

Understanding
Business on the
Internet
in a week

BOB NORTON
CATHY SMITH

Hodder & Stoughton

EADLINE GROUP

Order queries; please contact Bookpoint Ltd, 39 Milton Park, Abingdon, Oxon
OX14 4TD. Telephone: (44) 01235 400414, Fax: (44) 01235 400454. Lines are
open from 9.00 - 6.00, Monday to Saturday, with a 24 hour message answering
service. Email address: orders@bookpoint.co.uk

British Library Cataloguing in Publication Data
A catalogue record for this title is available from the British Library

ISBN 0 340 70540X

First published 1996
Second edition 1998
Impression number 10 9   8   7   6   5   4   3   2   1
Year   2003 2002 2001 2000 1999 1998

Cover photo from Zefa Photo Library

Typeset by Multiplex Techniques
Printed in Great Britain for Hodder & Stoughton Educational, a division of
Hodder Headline Plc, 338 Euston Road, London NW1 3BH by Cox & Wyman
Ltd, Reading.

■ I N T R O D U C T I O N ■

Until the early 1990s, the Internet was known about and used mainly by academics and computer enthusiasts. There is now a much wider interest, especially from the business community, as the Internet begins to provide greater opportunities for communication, information gathering, marketing and business transactions.

Understanding Business on the Internet in a Week explains in a non-technical way why managers need to understand what the Internet is and how it could change the way they do business.

We shall look at:

Sunday	What is the Internet?
Monday	How to get access
Tuesday	Electronic mail: communications and contacts
Wednesday	Finding your way around
Thursday	Resources, uses and benefits
Friday	Marketing on the Internet
Saturday	Issues for managers

Understanding Business on the Internet in a Week offers a practical, introductory guide to a force which managers should not ignore, even if they do not use it, and on which they should make informed judgements.

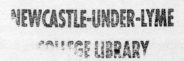

What is the Internet?

There are ten questions which people ask most about the
Internet. We shall deal with each of these in turn.

- What is the Internet?
- Is it the same as the Information Superhighway?
- How did the Internet start?
- Who can use it?
- How do I use it?
- How much will it cost?
- What can I do and find on the Internet?
- Can I access anybody's information anywhere?
- How do I find this information?
- What's in it for business?

What is the Internet?

Firstly, what is it not? The Internet is not a supercomputer
bringing everything together in one central location. It is a
worldwide network of computer networks which are
connected to each other by telecommunications links. The
network is made up of a variety of organisations, including
government departments, universities and commercial
companies which have decided to allow others to connect to
their computers and share their information. It is up to each
organisation how much data they make available and on
what basis. In return they can use the information of other
organisations. There is no owner of the Internet. The
nearest thing to a governing body is a number of voluntary
organisations, such as the Internet Society or the Internet
Engineering Taskforce.

Is it the same as the Information Superhighway?

There are several definitions of the superhighway. To some the Internet *is* the superhighway, while to others the superhighway means better telephone and cable lines to support the Internet. To another group, the superhighway will be more than the Internet, combining various communications links including telephone, wireless and satellite. Another view is that the Internet is developing into the superhighway as it becomes an effective and secure medium for business.

How did the Internet start?

The Internet started in the 1960s when the United States military decided it needed a secure means of moving its information around the world. It set up a series of computer links (known as ARPANet) so that it did not have to rely on

one route for its intelligence. This meant that if, for any
reason, data was prevented from travelling in one direction
it would find its way to its destination via another. It also
ensured that the defence intelligence system could not easily
be put out of action.

Academics soon saw the potential of the Internet for
communicating with each other and exchanging research
and ideas. Early computer enthusiasts also welcomed its
vast possibilities for similar reasons. And there it stayed for
twenty years, well known and used by these three groups –
the military, the academics and the nerds or anoraks as the
computer people came to be labelled. The Internet
continued to be most heavily used in and influenced by the
United States, although it rapidly came to be a worldwide
community. In the 1980s, large companies started to use the
Internet and in the 1990s, businesses of all kinds began to
get connected. Networks in ninety countries now make up
the Internet and this number is growing rapidly.

Who can use it?

Anybody who has a personal computer. Academics and computer enthusiasts have always been big users but there are just as many business people and ordinary consumers now. People either use the Internet to help them in their work, or at home for their hobbies, or to communicate with others, or a mix of all three.

How do I use it ?

You need a computer which can link to a network which is part of the Internet. Your organisation might be on the Internet in which case you can take advantage of a permanent connection. Most people's means of connection, however, is to subscribe to one of the commercial organisations which are willing to let you use their computer on the Internet for a fee. These firms, known as Internet Access Providers, offer access to the Internet via a telephone call, usually to a local number.

This is a very cheap means of using the Internet and has largely accounted for the phenomenal growth in interest in it. This is particularly true in North America where local calls are free in some areas. It is impossible to say how many users there are on the Internet but in 1997 it was estimated that there were over 12 million machines and over 60 million users. Tomorrow you will find out more about how to get access.

How much will it cost?

The costs fall into two categories: set-up and usage. You will need a personal computer with a modem. A modem is a card which sits inside the computer and turns your data input into digital signals which can be carried along normal telephone lines. These digital signals are called packets and they each contain the address label of their destination.

You will also need an arrangement with an Internet Access Provider. This company will usually charge you a one-off signing-on fee as well as a monthly usage subscription. In addition, because the Internet traffic is carried on telecommunications lines, you will have to pay telecoms connection charges, usually at the rate of a local call. Another cost of usage, that of your time, is difficult to predict because it will depend on how hooked you become: beware, the Internet is a notorious gobbler-up of time. Half an hour a day is a conservative estimate and then you have to add on the time you spend reading about it and keeping up to date with new information available and other developments.

In the past there have been few places to spend money on the Internet, because there has been no secure means of making and receiving payments. This will rapidly change, however, as the facilities become available and users begin to trust them.

You will hear more of this as we go through the week. Most computers allow you to use their information free of charge, although some are password protected, which means that you have to have prior authorisation to use the facilities.

What can I do and find on the Internet?

There are three main functions on the Internet: communication, information gathering and marketing.

Communication
The Internet is mostly used for communication and this is in the form of electronic mail. Email, as it is more popularly known, is the ability to send and receive electronic messages. Each email account on the Internet has a unique address code which allows the messages to be sent to the correct location. An email message is typed like a letter but can be received immediately like a telephone call.

Messages can be sent not only to people you know but also to people you haven't met. Special interest groups set up on the Internet allow the exchange of ideas, via email, with unknown colleagues who have similar interests. Questions can be asked of unknown experts and answers received within hours. Turn to Tuesday to find out more about email.

Information gathering
Information is available on a myriad of topics, in a variety of forms, including library holdings, product and market information, government statistics, paintings in art galleries, computer software, details of pop stars' latest albums and tours, recipes, weather reports and travel information. This

information is found on the World Wide Web (WWW). The WWW is an application which allows users to view a file of text and/or graphics and move to another file by means of links established between them. It is worth remembering that this information, at the moment, largely excludes that which organisations want you to pay for and that sources can appear and disappear overnight. Turn to Thursday for more on the range of information on the Internet.

There is, however, another side to the Internet. As well as these legitimate items, anyone can also find out how to make bombs or perpetrate credit card fraud or look at pornographic material on the World Wide Web.

Marketing
Anything from flowers to professional organisations or software is marketed on the World Wide Web.

Some adverts are very professional, others amateurish, but all are experimental. The best provide you with useful information as they market to you. Skip to Friday for more on marketing.

Can I access anybody's information anywhere?

You can only access what others have chosen to make available. To protect data they don't want you to see, they put it behind a security wall or 'firewall', as it is known. Nothing guarantees 100% security, however, short of having two organisational networks: one on the Internet and one outside, each entirely independent of the other. See Saturday for further security issues and developments.

How do I find this information?

It can be very difficult to track what is available on the Internet and, because of the ever-increasing amount of traffic, it can be a slow process to reach the computer where the information you want is held.

You need to know the address of the computer on the WWW which holds the information you want, just as you need to know the email address of a colleague to whom you want to send a message. There are finding tools on the Internet but the majority of these can be time-consuming to use, partly because of the vast amount of information they have to cope with. Turn to Wednesday for more on finding your way around.

An easy way to track information you might be interested in is to scan the daily newspapers and journals or magazines in your work or hobby-related subject area and record any addresses you think may be useful. There will certainly be some.

What's in it for business?

Commercial bodies recognised the possibilities of the Internet in the 1990s. This interest was fuelled by the growth in the use of the Internet which was prompted by three main factors: the rise in the sales of personal computers, the development of the WWW which replaced cumbersome searching and navigating mechanisms with a graphical interface, and the discovery and promotion of the Internet by the media. The business community realised that here was a massive market to be tapped.

Business initially hit a problem in that the Internet community had developed its own code of ethics. In a sense it had become a network of special interest groups which operated on a mutual help and exchange basis for no commercial gain. Early attempts by commerce to sell products or services on the Internet were met by extreme anger and hostility from the Internet community. One firm which tried was hounded off the network.

It is now routine for commercial organisations, big or small, to market on the Internet. This has been made possible in large part by the advent of the WWW which has made professional, and not so professional, marketing easy and cheap to achieve. Marketing is covered in greater detail on Friday, and Saturday will deal with related business and management issues.

Ten things you can do on the Internet

- Ask questions of unknown experts
- Email the White House
- Buy a book
- Find out about company products
- Transfer software updates
- Search the library of Congress
- Check airline flight schedules
- Look at the Mona Lisa
- Find out the Budget details
- Follow a training course

Good and bad things about the Internet

It:

- Is democratic
- Enables cheap and efficient long-distance communication
- Is great for personal networking
- Has worldwide marketing potential
- Opens up worldwide sources of information
- Has found a user friendly interface in the World Wide Web

But also it:

- Is chaotic and can be slow
- Threatens users with information overload
- Is time-consuming
- Offers few guarantees of security or confidentiality
- Carries illegal, unsuitable or trivial information
- Changes every day

Summary

Today we have looked at what the Internet is, touching on its advantages and disadvantages. There are several steps which you can take to increase your knowledge:

- Read the daily press and journals in your professional area
- Talk to colleagues and friends
- Try and see a demonstration of the Internet or get half an hour's time to experiment
- Watch out for workshops in your geographical or subject area

Tomorrow we will look at the various issues involved in getting access.

How to get access

Today we will learn more about getting the appropriate connection for access to the Internet.

There are two main ways of access: through an organisational network and a leased line (known as full access) or via a dial-up connection to an Internet Access Provider. We shall look at:

- Full network access
- Dial-up access
- How to choose an Internet Access Provider

Full network access

Your organisation is only likely to have full network access if it has an Information Technology (IT) department, because a fair amount of technical work is involved in setting up and maintaining a permanent link to the Internet. This link consists of a computer, a physical cable supplied by a telecoms company, such as British Telecom (BT), and a box called a router (defined in the resource requirements list below). Your connection, which will be open all the time, is likely to be to one of the backbone networks, such as Super Janet in the United Kingdom, Ebone in Europe or the American National Science Foundation's NSFNet in the United States. Most of these networks have been publicly funded but there are some commercial ventures.

Your first step, therefore, is to check with the IT department to see if it maintains a full-time link. If it does, ask if you can take advantage of it. Find out if there is any training available for new Internet users and, if not, talk to colleagues who have learnt to use the Internet and see if they are willing to pass on the benefit of their experience.

Benefits of full access
These are some of the advantages which a computer network with full access to the Internet has over an individual personal computer with dial-up access:

- A much faster capability of sending and receiving information
- Superior electronic mail capability
- Control and independence

Resource requirements
If your organisation does not have full access, consider the costs carefully before you recommend this option. You will need:

- A computer (or server as it is usually termed). It should be quite a powerful machine to handle incoming and outgoing traffic
- A router, which allows data signals from your network to be sent to other networks. Depending on the amount of traffic, an organisation may have more than one router Internet Access Providers, for example, have several
- A firewall, which is a computer that sits between the Internet and your computer network acting as a device to keep intruders at bay

- A dedicated, leased line from your network to another network on the Internet, which will entail an installation and annual rental fee of significant proportions. It can be supplied directly by all the main telecoms companies, such as BT, Mercury, or Energis, or by the cable operators, or installed by an Internet Access Provider. You will need to decide on the bandwidth you want. (Bandwidth dictates the speed at which data can be carried on the line. A useful analogy is the varying speeds at which water can move, depending on the width of the pipe.) A fairly basic line (64kbps) will cost in the region of £10,000 per annum
- Staff to set up and maintain your link

Of course, you may already have the equipment and staff available if they are employed for other functions; if so these costs will be greatly reduced or more easily absorbed.

Dial-up access

Usually only large organisations have a full link to the Internet, so most people access it via what is called a dial-up connection from their personal computer (PC) to a commercial Internet Access Provider. This is not a permanent connection, as with full access, but is only active when you dial-up (as in making an ordinary telephone call) to the provider's host computer.

Equipment checklist for dial-up access
You will need:

- A personal computer. It is difficult to outline a specification for a suitable state-of-the-art PC for Internet access when technological progress is so rapid. At the time of writing, however, a 486 SX 33 megahertz is adequate, but a pentium is preferable. It is advisable to have an expandable memory capacity which will enhance your capability to transfer and download files
- A telephone line and a modem. It doesn't matter if you use a direct line or have to dial out via a switchboard, but have a dedicated socket. If you are buying a new PC, have the modem built in as part of the package. The speed of data transmission down the telephone lines will depend on the speed of the modem you use. A modem sending and receiving data at 28.8 bits per second is suitable, but 33.6 or 56 are faster options. Do check that your chosen Internet Access Provider can take the speed of modem connection which you wish to use
- An ISDN line and an adaptor. Instead of using a standard telephone line and modem you can use an ISDN line and a piece of hardware called an adaptor. It is a more expensive option but provides faster, better quality access

- Internet access software. This has all the functionality needed to carry out tasks on the Internet, such as an email package and a browser for the WWW. Providers generally send you the software on disk through the post
- An account with an Internet Access Provider. Companies offering Internet access have mushroomed and offer varying rates and services. Later today we look at various aspects to consider when choosing a provider. Telephone numbers of some of the UK providers are given at the end of this chapter

Access problems

Dial-up access is very cheap (see the following section on costs) but is subject to the vagaries of what is happening on the data lines or on the remote host computer which allows you Internet access. It is important to recognise that things can and will go wrong from time to time. Some of the disadvantages are summarised below:

- As the connection isn't permanent, electronic mail which is sent to you doesn't come straight to your computer. You have to dial-up and collect it from the provider
- Access can be slow (but is improved with faster modem speeds)
- The host computer is sometimes unavailable because of maintenance or other difficulties

- Providers can get overloaded because of the sheer number of users, particularly first thing in the morning. The data lines can get very busy in the afternoon when North America is awake

Costs
There are two kinds of charges you pay for a dial-up connection:

- Internet Access Provider fees. These usually include a one-off signing-on fee plus a flat rate fee for unlimited monthly usage. £200 per annum is a standard charge at 1997/8 prices

- Telecoms charges. You will also incur these charges as you are using the telephone lines to reach the provider. They can soon mount up, so in order to reduce them, the Internet providers offer contact telephone numbers or, in Internet parlance, 'Points of Presence' (PoPs) around the country. The idea is that any user should only need to contact a local number and pay a local call rate. Some providers offer local PoPs around the country, others specialise in a local area

How to choose an Internet Access Provider

Providers quickly earn a reputation for what they offer. Consider the factors listed below and ask other users what their experience of various providers has been.

1.   *Try out the service*
Can you try the service before you buy it? This might be possible at an exhibition (there is a large Internet exhibition held in London every Spring) or at a seminar (there are plenty of hands-on training workshops available). There are now several Cybercafés around the UK where you can buy a cappuccino and have half an hour, or an hour's trial on the Internet very cheaply. Look out for offers where you can explore the Internet free of charge for a period.

2.   *Check the fee rates*
Find out the various fee structures. Be wary of special deals, such as the waiving of the signing-on fee, which are sometimes used to promote a particular supplier.

3.   Assess the ease of use of the software and what it contains
Find out how easy and time-consuming it is to install the
software. Will you be able to install it yourself or will you
require assistance from a friend or colleague or even from a
specialist? Check that you will be sent up-to-date versions of
the software.

4.   Ensure that adequate support is available
Does the provider have a help desk number? If so, how
easy is it to get through to? How helpful and friendly are the
staff? Some providers seem to assume that users are already
skilled computer users.

Most providers include help files in the software but these
can be unintelligible to the novice or do not seem to contain
the information you need.

5.   Ask about free Web space
Some providers give up to 5 megabytes of free space on
their server to allow you to build your own Web site. Find
out how much space they are offering, how much it would
cost to rent more if needed now or later, and whether there
are any restrictions on usage.

6.   Enquire about your own domain name
The provider will give you a email address, usually in the
form: yourname@providername.co.uk If you are taking out
an account for an organisation, ask if you can have an
address which reflects that organisation's name instead.
(This is referred to as having your own domain name.) The
provider will charge you an additional fee to register your
domain name. See Tuesday for a further explanation of
email addresses.

7.   Investigate the provider's reputation

Try and find out any background information on the
providers, for example, has there been any transfer of
personnel around the providers or do any of them have
powerful partnerships with other companies to help them
provide the service?

Internet Access Providers

These are the names and telephone numbers of some of the
many companies offering Internet access in the United
Kingdom:

BTnet:	0345 585110
CityScape:	01223 566950
Cix:	0181 255 5050
Demon:	0181 371 1234
Easynet:	0171 681 4321
Pipex:	0500 474739
PSI Net UK:	01223 577167
UK Online:	01749 333333

Microsoft's Windows95 includes an application called Microsoft Network. This gives users access to the Internet, subject to registration and giving credit card details.

Training providers
Many organisations offer regular or one-off Internet training courses. Find out what is available in your geographical area by consulting the local press, colleges, TEC or Chamber of Commerce. Check what is offered in your subject area by monitoring the professional journals.

Summary

Today we have looked at the equipment you will need for full and dial-up access and advised you to take a little time in choosing an Internet Access Provider, asking the views of existing users if possible. Tomorrow we will look at sending and receiving electronic mail, the first steps most people take on the Internet.

Electronic mail: communications and contacts

Electronic mail is the most widely used function on the
Internet. Best estimates put email use at 85% of all Internet
traffic. Companies offering email facilities have been
around for several years but the interest in and use of email
has really grown because the Internet has made it much
cheaper to use and because high-speed, efficient and low-
cost modems, which are necessary to relay it, have become
available. Today we look at:

- What is electronic mail?
- Email addresses
- Netiquette
- Newsgroups and discussion lists
- Managers' thoughts on email
- Advantages and disadvantages of email

What is electronic mail?

Electronic mail, or email as it is more commonly known, is
an electronic cross between letters, telephone calls and faxes.

- Like a letter an email message has to be written
  down but it can be informal like a telephone call
- Like a telephone call it is sent along the telephone
  lines but is split into 'packets' which may travel by a
  variety of routes and is then put together again at its
  destination

- Like a fax, but unlike a telephone call, it can be sent at a time convenient to the sender and read at a time convenient to the recipient. This is particularly useful where the correspondents are in different time zones or where it avoids the recipient being interrupted by the message, in the case of a sales person with a customer, for example
- Like a telephone call it is a very immediate form of communication but with the mixed blessing that your thoughts are in writing
- Unlike a telephone call it does not allow simultaneous two-way communication, although messages can bounce forwards and backwards very quickly, giving a conversation of sorts. Another internet function, Internet Relay Chat, does enable real-time conversation with a remote user but it can be a slow and laborious process
- Like a fax or letter it can handle not only text but also graphics

- Like a fax, messages can be relayed from one to one, or one to many, with only one copy of the original document
- Like a letter, fax or telephone call you need to know the address of the person to whom you are sending a message. However, it is also possible to send messages to a group of people where you know their collective address but not their individual ones. This latter facility, where people with the same interests set up what are called newsgroups or discussion lists, gives email users great power, permitting them to exchange information and opinions with people they have never met
- Email users do not have to be at home or at their desk to read their messages; all they need to do is to dial into their Internet Access Provider. An email address means you are not tied to a place to access it, like a traditional postal address

Users in organisations which have the advantage of full Internet access have email sent straight to their PC or terminal so that they are alerted to new messages when they log in or as they are working. They can also send messages as soon as they are written. Dial-up users experience a delay as they must connect to their Internet Access Provider to collect and receive their email. The most economical way to use email for a dial-up Internet user is to read and write messages off-line (i.e. when you are not connected to the Internet Access Provider) and only go on-line (connect) when you want to collect or send messages.

Email addresses

Each person using email on the Internet has a unique address which has several parts to it. For example,

bloggs_j@easynet.co.uk

is made up in the following way:

bloggs_j – the computer username of the user

@ – 'is found at'

easynet – the name of the host computer which is on the Internet

co – the type of organisation which owns the host computer, in this case a company, but there are also other codes, such as *ac* for academic organisations, *org* for non-profit making organisations and *gov* for government departments and agencies. (These codes may vary from country to country. For example, in the United States, *ac* is replaced by *edu*)

uk – the country code. All countries have a code except the USA where the Internet started.

Other examples of addresses include:

president@whitehouse.gov

santa@north.pole.org

institute@easynet.co.uk

Don't be surprised if you sometimes come across addresses that look different. These will be based at email services which used to be outside the Internet. For example, 70006.101@compuserve.com, is the customer service address for CompuServe which has long provided business and private individuals with access to email and database, and latterly, Internet facilities.

Finding addresses
There are email address directories available, but with such rapid growth in email usage, their coverage can only be patchy at best. The practical option is to build up your own directory over time by collecting those addressses which you use regularly, or those which may be useful at some stage. These can be found on email you receive, for example, or on business cards, in the press and on the radio and television. Telephoning or faxing people for their email address is accepted practice. Remember that everyone else is in the same boat so help them by publicising your own address.

Netiquette

As we have mentioned, email is a very immediate form of communication which allows you to write in haste and regret at your leisure. To try and mitigate this and to overcome the limitations of a medium which does not allow for normal visual and audio reactions, a system of Internet etiquette, or 'netiquette' as it has been dubbed, has evolved. Use of capital letters denotes SHOUTING or ANGER. A list of characters known as 'smileys' are used to give extra meaning to words, for example

   :-) means that the writer is happy
   ;-) is a wink and a smile.

Abbreviations are also popular, for example:

AISI	As I see it
BTW	By the way
HTH	Hope this helps
IMHO	In my humble opinion
FAQ	Frequently asked/answered question
FYI	For your information.

Newsgroups and discussion lists

Suppose you would like to correspond with others who share your leisure and work interests but you are not sure where to find them. Email allows you to join newsgroups or discussion lists where like-minded people swap news, gossip, discuss new developments, ask each other questions and send information and advice. This is done by sending a message to the group's email address and this gets passed on to everyone else in the group and you get everyone else's messages in return. You can be a part of a group for as short or as long a time as you like. You can be entirely passive and just read the messages which come in or take an active part by forwarding messages.

Newsgroups

A listing of the newsgroups available appears in most providers' software and it is fairly straightforward to select those that you wish to take part in. Beware though, once you join a group you can receive tens or hundreds of messages a day so don't be too enthusiastic in joining too many at first. Depending on the software you use, either all messages will be downloaded from the Internet Access Provider's computer each time you log in or you can run through the list of what is available at that time and choose to download only those which you wish to read in detail.

Examples of newsgroups

The following give you a flavour of the newsgroups available (alt. just means 'alternative'; misc. stands for miscellaneous; and rec. is short for 'recreation'):

```
alt.fan.madonna
alt.education.research
alt.business.seminars
alt.management.tech-support
alt.alien.research
misc.business.consulting
misc.entrepreneurs
rec.autos.sport.f1
rec.music.classical
```

Discussion lists

Discussion lists work in a slightly different way and tend to be more specialised and for a smaller group of people. They are often moderated which means that they are overseen by one or more people who control what goes through to the list. This is a way, for example, of filtering out unwelcome adverts from individuals and companies wishing to sell their products or services. On occasions when adverts do get through to a list, it is common for the originators to be 'flamed', that is receive a reply containing a strong opinion that the message is unwelcome. When tens and hundreds of people do this the offender's computer can grind to a halt.

Discussion lists are a good forum for clubs, groups and committees to keep in touch, receive minutes of meetings and exchange information.

Examples of discussion lists

> *bpr-l*   Business process reengineering
> *hrnet*   Human resources network
> *learning-org*   Learning organisation
> *leadrshp*   Leaders and leadership
> *management-research*   Management research
> *trdev-l*   Training and development
> *telework*   Teleworking

The authoritative guide to discussion lists is *The Directory of Scholarly and Professional Electronic Conferences* by Diane Kovacs. This is available from the United States Association of Research Libraries or via the Internet in various forms.

Managers' thoughts on email

'My initial email activity has been to correspond with friends and ex-colleagues who are not within easy reach.'

'Here everybody uses email as much as possible, thus reducing the amount of paper used. It is a very efficient way of checking what is going on and you do not risk losing an important note or report. You receive the information very fast and can act very fast too. It is also cheaper than using the phone. It's fun just to be able to communicate so easily with all sorts of people.'

'Whenever I have placed a request for help on one of the newsgroups I have usually had the correct answer within twenty-four hours.'

'Whilst communicating around the newsgroups I have built up a friendship with people around the world.'

'We use email a lot; I receive forty-plus messages daily, from countries such as the USA, Australia and Germany and sometimes from Turkey and Russia.'

'I set up as a consultant last year. My email address allows me to talk to my clients (many large companies now have email). I also subscribe to a number of newsgroups which keep me appraised of professional developments as well as providing a network of contacts.'

'I am using email to swap data between the various companies in our group. We are an international company. Using a mail box means we are not tied to any routine or physical presence.'

'I joined primarily to be able to send electronic mail to my daughter at university.'

Advantages and disadvantages of email

Advantages
- Delivery is faster than traditional mail or 'snail mail' as email users like to call it
- It overcomes time zone differences as the recipient does not have to be available to receive it
- One-to-many correspondence is simple
- An email address is portable
- It enables you to exchange information with people previously unknown to you
- As the information is carried in electronic form it can easily be reused
- The cost is not dependent on the distance the message has to travel
- It is much cheaper than fax or telephone
- Replying to messages is straightforward because the reply facility includes the originator's address

Disadvantages
- It is not very secure; anyone can intercept and read your email if they really want to
- Devotees can become over-exuberant in its use and bombard you regularly, some with long, rambling messages

- Sometimes the apparent immediacy of email, like fax, can panic you into thinking that you need to respond straight away. Unlike a letter, the immediacy can take over
- It can be used inappropriately, for example, a long document, unless urgent, is better posted in the traditional way thereby saving the recipient's time and paper in printing it out
- You can become a postbox for other people who do not have an email account but have friends and contacts who do
- It encourages off-the-cuff replies which you may regret later
- Printouts of email can look rather untidy; this is most likely to occur when you are sending to a mail system which is different from the one you use

Summary

Today we have looked at how email works, what it is used for and its advantages and disadvantages. As well as communication, it is a way of finding information. Other ways of finding information on the Internet will be considered tomorrow.

Finding your way around

There is so much information available on the Internet that it is easy to flounder about and get confused.

Today we highlight the main functions available, other than email, and give some pointers on how you can find your way around. We shall look at:

- Searching databases (Telnet)
- Transferring files from one computer to another (FTP)
- Using the World Wide Web
- Search tools
- A map of the Internet

We shall particularly concentrate on the World Wide Web. Apart from email, this is the part of the Internet which is easiest to use and is the most useful for business.

Searching databases (Telnet)

The Internet gives you the opportunity to search databases, such as library catalogues, using either the Telnet protocol or the WWW. Telnet allows you to enter the address of the computer you want to visit and log in as an anonymous user. Some computers are password protected which means that you need to register with the organisation beforehand. Telnet merely takes you to the host computer; once there, you are inside the environment of the host computer and therefore subject to its own search language. Today, Telnet has largely been superseded by the WWW; most organisations offer a Web interface to their database.

Transferring files from one computer to another (FTP)

Thousands of computers on the Internet have files which are freely available to the public.

These range from computer programs to the text of Alice in Wonderland.

If you wish to retrieve a file, you need to use a file transfer protocol (usually referred to as FTP) which ensures that data stored on one computer can be transmitted to another. You need to know the address of the computer which holds the file you require, log in using 'anonymous' as your username and generally your email address as your password, and then transfer the file. It is also possible, and easier, to transfer files using the WWW.

There are some major FTP sites around the world: the main one in the UK is at Imperial College, London *(ftp:// sunsite.doc.ic.ac.uk)*.

If you have a WWW site, you use FTP to transfer new and updated pages to the server where your site is held. In this case, you are sending files, rather than getting them.

Using the World Wide Web (WWW)

The Web has done much to reduce the mystery of the Internet and transform it into a useable resource. It is a programme which cross references, links and retrieves data from computers around the world using what is called a hypertext system. This allows you to move from one document to another using a mouse to click on highlighted terms or graphics. The moves are seamless, enabling you to find information in all forms: graphics, video and sound as well as text. The information you will find on the WWW is extraordinarily diverse as anyone with a computer, modem and a little expertise can set up a Web page. You can see the jokes and family snapshots of Joe Bloggs side by side with data from the CIA and NASA.

All documents on the WWW have a unique address, known as a Uniform Resource Locator (URL), which has several parts to it. For example, Sainsbury's address is: http:// www.j-sainsbury.co.uk and is made up as follows:

> *http://* – hypertext transfer protocol
> *www.j-sainsbury.co.uk* – the name of the server,
>   including the organisation's name, type and country
>   of origin

In some cases a file name may be specified. In that case a slash(/) would be used to separate the file name from the directory name.

Other protocols can also be used on the Web such as *ftp://* and *telnet://*.

To use the World Wide Web you need a browser. This is a piece of software which views the information contents of other sites on the Web and enables quick transfer – or hyperlinks – from one page to another and from one site to another. It also allows you to download (copy) any pages you wish to store on hard disc to see or print later.

The browser is usually supplied by the Internet Access Provider. Two browsers have emerged as market leaders; one is Netscape, the other is Microsoft's Explorer. Both are subject to regular improvements and upgrades. Many Website pages have been designed with one particular browser in mind, which means that you may have problems if you are using a different one.

Search tools

A major headache is finding out what information is available and where it is located. The tools listed below are, we suggest, last resorts as they can be time-consuming to use and will turn up many sources of information. A search on general management will yield thousands of potential sites to visit, for example. Other more comfortable ways of identifying sources of information include the press, the professional journals in your subject area and recommendations from friends and colleagues. Do bear in mind, however, that there is constant change on the Internet. Addresses can change and sites can appear overnight and disappear just as quickly.

DejaNews
As we have said, newsgroups can be an excellent source of
expertise and specialist knowledge, but there are thousands
of them. At the time of writing, DejaNews is acknowledged
as a primary newsgroup searcher which identifies the
subjects of more than 20,000 newsgroups
(*http://www.dejanews.com/*).

Gopher and Archie
A way of identifying which FTP files and remote databases
are available is by using a tool called Gopher. A Gopher is a
computer program which organises files in a standard menu
format in order to browse the contents. Another search
system for FTP files is called Archie, which allows you to
scan indexes to the major FTP sites.

Search engines and directories

With hundreds of thousands of organisations and individuals putting up information on the WWW, a printed directory of the contents is not feasible. Instead you use finding tools on the Web itself to locate the information you want. These tools are known as directories or search engines. Directories are created by people who evaluate and index vast amounts of new material on a continuous basis. Probably the best known is Yahoo! Search engines are created by software programmes designed to trawl continuously through Web sites for new information and automatically add new sites and pages to a database. This helps to explain why you can get large amounts of dross along with significant items of interest; search engines are indiscriminate and non-evaluative – they trawl every day and put up everything available. The best known is WebCrawler.

There are hundreds of directories and search engines available and they vary in the type of search they offer, in ease of use and in the speed and efficiency of their retrieval of information. It is worth trying the same search in two or three of them as they may well have recorded information in different ways. Bear in mind that although this will increase your potential for finding what you want, it will also increase the overall number of 'hits' and inevitably include at least some dross. Here are some directories and search engines for tackling information finding on the Web.

- Hotbot *(http://www.hotbot.com/)* – no need for any specialist search skills and allows you to narrow your search requirements to, for example, the last week
- Altavista (http://www.altavista.digital.com/) – claims more than 27 million hits per day; popular, fast and simple, and shows topics of related interest
- Lycos *(http://www.lycos.com/)* – enables search refinement and limiting the number of hits; includes free classified advertising, financial news, maps and city guides
- Excite *(http://www.excite.com/)* – allows tracking of up to 20 search topics from 300, (mainly American) publications, for tailoring new information to your personal needs
- Infoseek *(http://www.infoseek.com/)* – eliminates duplicate hits from more than 100,000,000 pages and has a specific UK directory
- Yahoo! UK and Ireland *(http://www.yahoo.co.uk/)* – a British/Irish derivative from a well-established directory which stands for 'Yet Another Hierarchical Organized Oracle'
- Galaxy *(http://www.einet.net/galaxy.html)* – aimed at business and professional users
- Metacrawler (http://www.metacrawler.com/) – allows you to access several major search engines and eliminates duplicate hits
- WebCrawler *(http://www.webcrawler.com)* – trawls the Web continuously and brings hundreds of thousands of documents in its net by tracking occurrences of terms from one document to another and from one computer to another

Sorting the Information

None of the search engines or directories are truly comprehensive. Such is the mass of information they now hold, however, that even if you are searching for a fairly common term, you could end up with hundreds, even thousands, of hits to scan.

One answer in sorting the wheat from the chaff lies in relevance ranking. Here the search engine has the mathematical capability of sorting the hits in order of the number of times your search term is found in the document retrieved. Although many search engines have this capability, some Web-site compilers (WebMasters) load their sites with an exaggerated number of terms to ensure their site comes near the top of the order.

Another solution is to locate sites which specialise in hyperlinking to others – not indiscriminately – but as a result of selection and evaluation. For example:

- The University of Nijenrode (*http://www.nijenrode.nl/nbr*) has compiled a list of business information sources
- The Institute of Management (*http://www.inst-mgt.org.uk*) is building a list of sites of management interest
- The British Council (*http://www.britcoun.org.uk*) is selecting sites to offer 'a window on Britain' for overseas 'visitors'

Map of the Internet

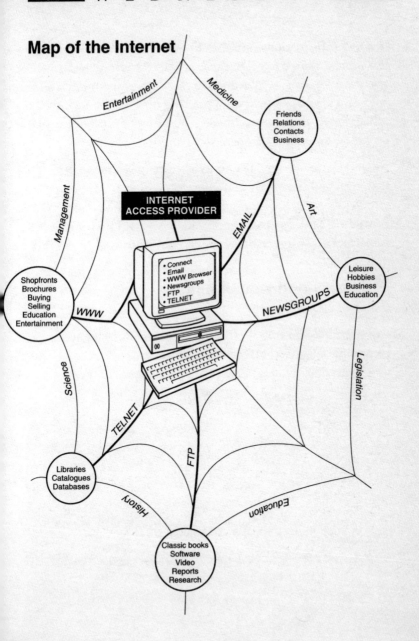

Because information continues to grow on a scale faster than the capability to control it, there is a need for intelligent agents, interfaces or intermediaries – both of the human and software kinds – to provide a filtering or selection facility which meets the needs of those who cannot afford hours of scanning time, or a hit-or-miss capability.

Intelligent agents enable you to identify new information suited to your needs by allowing you to set up your own profile; Excite is one example of this. Others learn from you by storing records of your previous visits and then suggest new information which may be of interest to you.

Summary and search hints

- The World Wide Web is the most widely used search and navigation tool on the Internet
- Search times and transmission speeds can be slow, especially in the afternoon (UK time) when both Europe and America are using the Internet
- You need patience as the painting of graphics can be particularly affected. Some sites indicate that you can dispense with graphics and opt for text only (and some browsers enable this). This will lose some of the visual impact but will speed the process of information flow especially if you are connected via a modem
- Be as precise in your search terminology as possible. If the term you are looking for is common, the likelihood is that the incidence rate will be very high

- When you find a useful site to which you will want to return, store the address in your browser to facilitate access next time
- There is continuous change on the Internet; sites appear and disappear rapidly

- Information on the Web is growing at a prolific rate. There is a need to adopt some ruthless selection and elimination procedures. Search tools continue to improve but still produce hits on a massive scale.

Tomorrow we will look at the type of information you can find on the Internet, how managers are using it and what benefits they derive.

Resources, uses and benefits

Now that we know how to get there and what's out there, what use are people making of the Internet? More importantly what benefits are they deriving? Today we shall look at:

- The resources that the Internet offers
- Ways of putting the Internet to use
- Case studies of managers' experiences

The resources that the Internet offers

There is quite simply a staggering amount of information which can only be measured in thousands of terabytes or millions of pages. It is a sobering thought that since the 1970s the world's output of information has grown exponentially, although it was as far back as 1830 that a scientist found he could no longer cope with all the new information relevant to his field. Most, if not all, of the information produced in recent years is in electronic form, and a large proportion of it is American in origin.

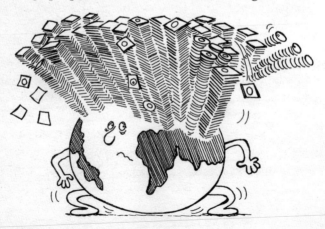

Another sobering thought is the democratic and anarchic character of the Internet where everyone's voice can be heard and everyone can be a publisher. Until recently the ethos of the Internet has been the free dissemination of thoughts and ideas as opposed to the evaluation and control usually found in commercially valuable or exploitable information.

That doesn't mean to say that the Internet can be easily ignored as a forum for the exchange of recipes and gardening tips. On the contrary.

There are a number of factors mitigating against rejection of all information sources on the Internet. The first and foremost is that it caters for a wide variety of personal, leisure and non-business activities. It is important to remember that the Internet widens the opportunity for pursuing these interests. Other reasons for taking the Internet seriously include a change in its culture as business and commercial interests become more involved, and the increase in the number of directional and selection tools.

These are a few examples of information sites that you can find on the Internet. Remember that they can change and disappear very rapidly!

Commercial organisations
Many corporate giants now offer value-added services to customers on the Internet, but it is not the exclusive domain of big business. It is as easy for small and medium-sized businesses to set up on the WWW; many of these have led the way and the giants have followed. Here are examples of just a few of the thousands of commercial organisations offering information and services:

Ford Motor Company *http://www.ford.co.uk*

Microsoft Corporation *http://www.microsoft.com*

J Sainsbury (company activities and initiatives; customer services including recipes and a direct wine purchasing service) *http://www.j-sainsbury.co.uk*

Virgin Atlantic (flight schedules, fare options and frequent flyer programmes) *http://www.fly.virgin.com*

The Halifax *http://www.halifax.co.uk*

Educational organisations
The MBA Page (prepared by the Fisher College of Business at Ohio State University to offer help and advice to MBA students) *http://www.cob.ohio-state.edu/dept/fin/ mba.htm*

Open University *http://www.open.ac.uk/*

Southampton Institute MBA *http://www.cecomm.co.uk/mba/index.html*

Virtual Online University *http://www.athena.edu*

Government bodies
NASA (space images) *http://images.jsc.nasa.gov/html/home.htm*

STAT-USA (from the US Department of Commerce; acts as an outlet for the US government's business, trade and economic information) *http://www.stat-usa.gov/*

Department of Trade and Industry *http://www.dti.gov.uk*

CCTA government information service *http://www.open. gov.uk*

UK government press releases (including those from the Bank of England, the Home Office, the Departments of Transport, the Environment, and Social Security and the Inland Revenue) *http://www.coi.gov.uk/coi/depts/deptlist.html*

UK government Treasury information *http://www.hm-treasury. gov.uk*

Office for National Statistics *http://www.ons.gov.uk*

Management
The Management Archive (forum for management ideas and information. Provides access to contributed working papers and preprints in the management and organisational sciences, course syllabi and teaching materials, conference announcements and archives of the Academy of Management.) *http://ursus.jun.alaska.edu*

Soundview Executive Book Summaries (includes abbreviated versions of the management book reviews that are published in hard copy. Other services include business questions and answers and management ideas of the week) *http:// www.summary.com*

Technology and Operations Management (this is a group at the Harvard Business School which includes links to working papers) *http://rigel.hbs.harvard.edu*

Uncover (on-line table of contents index and article delivery service for approximately 17,000 magazines and journals) *http:// www.carl.org/uncover/unchome.html*

The Press
The Economist *http://www.economist.com*

The Daily Telegraph *http://www.telegraph.co.uk*

Dow Jones News Service *http://www.dowjones.com*

Electronic Newsstand *http://www.enews.com*

The Financial Times *http://www.ft.com*

Harvard Business Review (abstracts of articles in current issue) *http://www.hbsp.harvard.edu*

Recreation
CarlingNet – official web site of the FA Carling Premiership
  http:// www.fa-premier.com

Movie Database *http://uk.imdb.com*

Rolling Stones *http://www.stones.com*

General interest
BBC *http://www.bbc.co.uk*

UK weather (Met office forecasts) *http://www.meto.govt.uk*

Travel advice notices from the Foreign and Commonwealth
  Office *http://www.fco.gov.uk/reference/travel_advice*

The London Guide (restaurants and pubs) *http://
  www.cs.ucl.ac.uk/misc/uk/london.html*

Paris Pages (What's new) *http://www.paris.org/whatsnew.html*

About New York City *http://www.ny.yahoo.com*

UK based WWW servers *http://src.doc.ic.ac.uk/all-uk.html*

UK rail timetables *http://www.railtrack.co.uk/travel*

Ways of putting the Internet to use

If most Internet traffic is for email, what is the rest for?
At the moment, accurate research on managers' use of the
Internet is still sketchy, partly because it is such a new

medium for most. Recent surveys of business use of the Internet have found, however, that significant numbers of respondents felt that the Internet had the potential to become a key tool for business operations and a growing proportion of users said it was currently contributing to their business. On the other hand, equally significant numbers were dissatified with it and believed it had been overhyped. While some claim to have 'no time for surfin', others are beginning to find it of value.

- Academics are using the Internet as a teaching medium with online conferencing, and as an information resource. They often create local discussion lists for students to use
- Publishers and authors are using email to transmit copy for the collation of magazines, to perform on-line editing and to cut down production time

- Small business and consultants are using appropriate newsgroups for kick-starting new projects by asking for help, advice or sources of information. Others trawl the 'wider' Internet for data sources and contact points listed in the web-crawlers we saw yesterday
- Organisations with international links use the Internet for cheap communications, staying in touch, news gathering on industries and competitors and seeking out collaborators
- Supermarkets are offering on-line ordering of groceries, and pizza houses allow you to create and order your own pizza over the Internet

- Many larger organisations are using the Internet to support telecommuting and working from home. In some cases, virtual businesses have been created where people may only meet face-to-face occasionally

- Transportation and tourism companies are using it for advance warning of traffic news, weather conditions and travel arrangements
- Museums are using the Internet to advertise exhibits and events by putting up full-colour images which users can download to their own PC
- Shopping malls have sprung up where flowers, books and goods of all sorts are sold
- One highly creative use is that of a bakery using the Internet to connect to weather forecasting services to determine what kind of produce to make available, rain or shine

Case studies of managers' experiences

The consultant

'I was able to use the Internet to access the virus name database of my software supplier on a Sunday afternoon, get an answer in a few minutes and reassure a worried client that she almost certainly did not have a virus on her computer. I had the option to download the latest anti-virus package if needed. I have obtained up-to-date printer drivers from both Microsoft and Hewlett Packard. I recently ordered various free catalogues from HMSO, browsing their database at leisure on a Sunday. I have discovered a lot of health-related information in the UK and elsewhere which will be useful. I accessed the US Department of Health to try to get some information on toxic chemicals and found a lot of data which will be valuable to a client in the future. The most useful service any company can provide via the

Internet in the first instance is to enable people to download their product data sheets. Clients nearly always want those yesterday.'

The management academic
'I'm a full-time management academic, but a part-time consultant and trainer also. I have in excess of forty associates and we use the Internet as our prime means of communication. As I largely work from home, email is a major means of communication with work colleagues and I have a growing number of contacts with students and friends outside the working environment. I also use the Internet as a teaching medium. We have a number of computer conferences and a course taught on- and off-line. Finally, the Internet provides a wider variety of research sources than I could previously access and this is a major saving of time and energy.'

The director and publisher
'I am the director of a games company as well as a management consultant. The magazine published by the company every month is built almost entirely of submissions transmitted across the Internet. Much of the news which we publish is gleaned from the Web and from newsgroups. These also give me access to a wide repository of expertise that is provided freely and enthusiastically.'

The market researcher

'The opportunity of carrying out market research on the Internet is exciting and frustrating. I had an assignment on the take-up of cable television and would have loved to have carried out a survey on the Internet. At the moment I'm writing a market research report on the catering industry and there appears to be no hard information about independent, outside caterers. I've also had an abortive attempt to shop on the Internet. The idea was good as my sister lives in New York and I thought I could order a present from a New York store via the Internet. One success though! A friend was going off to Moscow and I was able to use the weather information to get the Moscow report.'

The writer

'I have used the WWW to give me background knowledge of the cities my film star subjects lived in or visited during their lifetimes. For instance, one of my subjects lived for a time in West Hollywood and going into the West Hollywood Web page gave me information on the culture of the area as well as on the population of the city. The Internet also helped me build contacts in Los Angeles, where I travelled recently to carry out some research on my latest subject. I mailed a message to one of the newsgroups, asking for information about LA. I was contacted by an LA resident who emailed me advice and tips on how to get the best out of my visit.'

The software engineer

'We use the newsgroups to read about past experiences of
other people with particular products. For example, when
we needed to upgrade a PC, browsing the relevant
newsgroups indicated what hardware was "flavour of the
month". Practically all the computer products (hardware and
software) we now purchase are supported on Web pages.
This makes it easy to contact the manufacturer when
problems occur and the ability to download upgrades
ensures that we are always operating our equipment at
optimum levels. Finally, we develop software using the
compiler supplied by Borland. Recently, they had a
developers' conference in the United States and within a
couple of days the transcripts of the presentations were
available from their Web site which gave us information on
the strategic goals of the Borland compiler group.'

Summary

Today we have looked at the information available through the Internet and at the ways in which some managers are using it. Tomorrow we will look at how companies are using the Internet to market themselves and offer some advice on putting up information on your own organisation.

Marketing on the Internet

The Internet is a new marketing medium, full of promise but to be treated with some caution. It is wise to watch and learn from the experience and mistakes of others and to observe the ground rules which are emerging. Today we will tackle marketing on the Internet, mainly by concentrating on the World Wide Web. Marketing via Newsgroups can be done, but is still frowned on and so must be used with restraint. We ask:

- What have others done?
- Who's out there?
- What's different about it?
- Where do you start?
- What are the cost factors?
- What kind of marketing strategies can be used?
- What are the key criteria for success?

What have others done?

Early companies looking to market on the Internet found their heads turned by the worldwide market and barraged the newsgroups *en masse* with advertisements. But the tactic backfired. They were swamped with so many angry calls and complaints (or 'flames' as they are called by Internet users) that their computers were jammed and they promised not to do it again.

They were unfortunate in being the first to challenge the non-commercial ethos of the Internet and they failed to pay attention to targeting their adverts to those most likely to be interested.

However, these organisations were successful in that:

a) they got their message through
b) it was a very low-cost exercise compared to normal advertising
c) they did get replies.

Other organisations learnt the lessons of this experience and targeted a handful of newsgroups which might be especially interested in their product or service. Although they still got some flak, they began to benefit from the changing culture of the Internet and found it more receptive to marketing. They were less aggressive, more focused in their approach, ready and willing to take their time, and learn. And they have begun to pick up business.

The shift in stance towards marketing has taken place since the advent of the WWW. This has made it easy for firms to advertise and has allowed consumers to come to the advertising site rather than being bombarded with what they regard as junk mail.

One company launched a new product exclusively by means of the WWW. Within a couple of days, they received enquiries from all over the world, magazines called to run features on it, technical reviewers asked for a sample, and the company was asked to present their new product at an international conference.

Who's out there?

Accurate figures are not knowable but recent estimates have suggested that there are over 60 million Internet users worldwide, increasing by a million a month. In the UK alone, it is estimated that there are over 3,000,000 users, a figure which is rising fast. One commentator has projected that at current rates of growth everyone on the planet will be connected by the year 2003! Not all those who use the Internet, however, are potential customers, particularly if their Internet access is work-related and focused on communication.

The early profile of the Internet user was that of the ABC1 35-year-old male, described as literate, trend-setting and libertarian, who believes in freedom of speech and the right of every group to be heard.

The Internet 'trekkie', however, is becoming a less dominant character as business takes up use of the Internet. The 25–35-year-old company executive, interested in the possibilities of new technology, computer literate, and keen to explore the scope of electronic markets, constitutes a growing Internet user. The change has been described as a shift from 'anoraks' to 'suits'.

In reality, a mix of people use the Internet, for a wide variety of purposes, but that excludes large sectors of the population who are either less computer-literate than others, such as the retired, or those without easy access to computers, such as the unemployed.

What's different about it?

With the number of world-wide Web sites over 16,000,000 in 1997 and still rising, how do you exploit the Internet as a market-place? We have identified ten ground rules.

1. Electronic consumers cannot be treated like television viewers, newspaper readers or people looking at billboards. Newsgroup messages are not delivered to a person's letter-box like postal mail. Consumers log in

when they like, glance at the subject of messages, take what they like and ignore the rest. You will not know who has read your message unless they contact you. With a WWW site, again the consumer chooses where to visit and when, and for how long. However, the WWW does enable you to monitor the visitors.

2. As the user chooses to look at the organisation's information, the necessity to make it interesting and attractive is just as important as for TV- or paper-based advertising. Just as in the real world, Internet users have many claims on their attention and are becoming increasingly sophisticated and demanding.

3. There are almost no restrictions, apart from cost, to the amount of information you can make available. This availability is for twenty-four hours a day and on Sundays. The WWW does not close.

4. Because of the Internet's potential for reaching consumers on a hitherto unknown scale, the avoidance of brash marketing expletive and unsubstantiated hype is all the more important. If you make a promise you cannot deliver, thousands of people could know about it in minutes. An upset customer will quickly pass on dissatisfaction.

5. Electronic communications are interactive: recipients have a very easy facility for rapid reply, so marketing is no longer merely one-way. The sending organisation can, within minutes of transmission, receive a message saying 'don't send again', another complaining, another suggesting improvements and another expressing an interest in buying. If they have asked a question, they will expect a quick response. In the past the advertiser has invaded the consumer's living room; now the consumer can return the compliment.

Because of this two-way communication, the potential for building relationships with consumers, wherever they may be, is vastly increased.

6. The best WWW sites are those which are interesting, hold your attention, and have more to offer than marketing hype. They are updated to keep them fresh, alive and therefore attractive for people to revisit.

7. Exploitation of interactive media creates opportunities not only to attract by participation but also to learn about customer demographies, attitudes, wants, dislikes and behaviours, providing that the interaction is interesting and useful to the passer-by.

8. Small companies can now hope to reach an international market-place without the infrastructure of a huge multinational organisation. The Internet enables Jones & Co. to stand side by side with the Times Top 1000 in the market-place, competing for customers. With a possible market stretching from Alaska to Taiwan, and Scandinavia to Australia, remember that cultural differences and sensitivities will apply.

9. Market entry can be easy and low-cost on the Internet. This increases the need for businesses to track what others are doing.

10. Paying for products and services in a secure and confidential way will be resolved in the immediate future. Developments and experiments with electronic payments will be summarised on Saturday.

Where do you start?

Here are some guidelines on putting up pages on the World
Wide Web.

*1. Figure out if marketing on the Internet is suitable for you
and what your criteria for success are.*
One of the main attractions of the Internet is that it can
reach a far wider audience than by phone, letter,
conferences, exhibitions and mail-shot put together – a new
worldwide market unrestricted by the usual restrictions of
time, place and cost. It can be more difficult to target
particular groups this way, however. Take a look at
Developing an Internet Strategy on Saturday.

Decide on your objectives. Do you want to:

- Sign up new customers?
- Worry your competitors?
- Keep in touch with suppliers?

How will you measure success?

- Numbers of visits?
- Numbers of enquiries?
- Numbers of sign-ups/subscribers?
- Level of feedback?
- Features in the Press?

Remember that, as with all marketing efforts, gauging the contribution to the bottom line is problematic.

2. Look at what others have done.
Explore WWW sites – the shop-windows – of other organisations, including any similar to your own, and see what you like and what you don't. Look closely at the style and presentation of their layout, the typeface or font style, the use of colour, graphics and icons to catch the eye, the time taken for pages to appear, especially when they include still and moving images. Ask yourself if you are sufficiently interested to go back and look again, and why? Would you tell others about it? Is there anything you would wish to emulate, adopt, modify or reject?

3. Identify an Internet Access Provider to work with.

Renting space on a computer run by an Internet Access Provider is becoming an established method for getting onto the WWW. You can go it alone by setting up your own server, but this approach requires a more substantial investment in resources, skills and knowledge. The advantage of running your own server is the full and immediate control you gain in updating your pages and monitoring their usage. The disadvantage is the cost, not merely in the hardware to cater for many simultaneous users, but also in the technical resource needed to maintain and develop the system. Step back to Monday for a breakdown of the issues involved. At the moment using a server such as that offered by increasing numbers of providers is a cheaper, no-risk option. These companies include BTNet, Demon, Easynet, IBM Global Networks, and Pipex. There is also a growing number of independent Web publishing houses.

When selecting an Internet Access Provider bear in mind the following questions:

- What are their rates compared to those of others?
- How much are they willing to help and guide as part of their fee?
- If this help is limited, do they offer advice on constructing and designing pages on a consultancy basis?
- Do they provide regular reports on who visits your pages, when they visit, and how long they stay?
- What is their policy on updating the pages?
- Are they friendly and helpful?
- Do they use a language you can understand or is it all technobabble?
- Are they a quick, opportunistic start-up or have they been around for some time?
- Who else is using them and for which services?
- Do they have plans for introducing secure and confidential financial transactions? (Others will if they don't.)

4. Remember that the traditional requirements of innovation and creativity for quality advertising still apply.
Use a graphic designer if you can afford it, but make sure that the designer understands the medium of the Internet. Practices particularly appropriate to the content of WWW pages include:

- Making sure your branding or image remain consistent
- Giving value beyond marketing description so that customers will want to come back for information of regular interest such as latest bargain offers, direct booking at events or hotels, route maps and travel information, live updates of sporting or political events
- Making the pages clear, short and to the point, readable, unconfusing, free of jargon and waffle; there is a greater need for immediacy and brevity when people are paying for on-line time to look at your pages
- Keeping them up to date, new and fresh
- Avoiding too many graphics which take time to load on the screen and can be boring
- Providing imaginative links to enable customers to skip to related information instead of merely scrolling or turning pages; make it easy for people to find their way around
- Creating links to other computers such as those of collaborators, partners, suppliers, satisfied customers or related information sources; and from them to you
- Making it interactive by asking for feedback, comment and details of requirements; get customers to specify their own product preferences
- Making it expandable in the future

5. Make sure you try out your pages on a variety of browsers.
Different browsers can present the same information in
different ways. Check that your pages remain as you
intended them to look, especially on Netscape and Explorer.

6. Remember the two forms of access: full-access and dial-up.
Those with a leased line can handle graphics quicker than
those with dial-up. The latter may prefer a 'text only' version.
For information on dial-up access, look back to Monday.

What are the cost factors?

The cheapest form of advertising is to target specific
newsgroups but do use this approach with caution. It will
involve time in identifying the groups (see Tuesday),
writing suitable messages, sending them and receiving
replies. The time and cost spent in connection to the
Internet is minimal.

Unless your organisation is already part of the Internet, you
will have to rent space from an Internet Access Provider in
order to market on the WWW. The cost will depend on
factors such as:

- The amount of space you buy, usually quoted in
  megabytes, but translatable into pages and cheaper,
  year on year
- The amount of development work required on your
  information to structure it to work on the WWW,
  facilitated by programming packages such as Front
  Page to take away the labour-intensiveness
- The use of an experienced graphic designer familiar
  with the techniques needed for success on the Internet

- The levels of sophistication and use of graphics in design
- The numbers and types of hypertext links to other documents or sources on other computers
- The method and frequency of updating and refreshing it

At 1998 prices, a simple, straightforward 'shop-front' of a couple of pages would come perhaps to no more than a few hundred pounds. A site running to a hundred pages or more with greater sophistication and functionality including forms, various types of interactivity and clever links and connections could cost up to twenty or thirty thousand pounds to develop.

What kind of marketing strategies can be used?

If, as we have seen, brash advertising and overt aggression are to be avoided, what other kinds of marketing can be carried out on the Internet? Here are a few examples:

- Catalogues, company contacts and pricing information
- Product announcements and press releases
- Promotional notices of special sales
- Documentation and manuals
- Market research and customer surveys
- Reviews and service evaluations
- Customer service information

- Recruitment notices
- Dialogue with and involvement for the customer

Remember that the Internet enables two-way communication; interaction is the key to electronic marketing.

Summary

What are the key criteria for success?

- Decide what you want to achieve and how to measure it
- Decide whom you wish to target
- Don't rely too much on experience of the 'paper' medium
- Decide whether or not to employ a graphic designer
- Use graphics with care
- Keep your visitors interested with something new
- Try to get them involved
- Aim for consistency of 'look' and 'feel', particularly in branding
- Ask for statistics on who is looking at which page, when and how often

Having decided to market on the Internet, the next step would be to buy and sell services. How do you pay for goods on the Internet and what other business issues are there to be aware of?

These are the subjects for Saturday.

Issues for managers

We are in a period of transition where the Internet is no longer the exclusive preserve of academics and computer nerds. It is, however, not yet perceived as the dynamic medium in which business can have confidence for full commercial transactions, although that is clearly the direction in which it is rapidly moving.

So as managers make use of the Internet, what are the issues to be aware of? Today we will look at contentious and sometimes contradictory factors characterising the burgeoning information industry, which managers need to tackle. These concern:

- Managing time
- Managing people
- Managing information
- Managing finance
- Developing an Internet strategy

We are not suggesting that managers have an obligation to master the Internet through use of technical applications. But it is increasingly important to be aware of developments and keep up-to-date with changes through the daily and professional press because of the issues discussed here.

With commercial organisations, software houses and financial institutions putting substantial investment resources into the Internet, and with formerly separate technologies – data transmission, telecommunications, data compression, and the mix of text with sound, graphics and video – all successfully converging, opportunities or threats to business are presenting themselves faster than ever before. Progress in technical capability changes the picture every day as legislative bodies responsible for international law struggle to get to get to grips with the implications of information flow on a world-wide scale.

In the past, a technological future was always just around the corner. Now it is here.

Managing time

Good practice in time management is one of those things that is extremely well documented but nonetheless hard to achieve in reality. The problem is now being exacerbated by the masses of information available at the touch of a button.

Information overload

If information overload was a problem before, the Internet may make it worse. Coping tactics include:

- Learning the best sources for information, and how to access them, rather than trying to store it yourself
- Working out personal screening procedures e.g. culling by source of origin, or eliminating on subject or one-line headers
- Making use of relevance ranking which is available on more and more search engines
- Not overloading networks with garbage by passing on data which "might" be of interest to others
- Restricting yourself to 'needs' and 'musts' by sticking to objectives and asking yourself – when faced with a pile of unsolicited information – if you would have gone looking for it in the first place
- Thinking in terms of useable intelligence instead of potentially useful data
- Resorting to the delete key, and making the problem disappear!

The Curiosity Factor

There is a temptation to surf the world on the Web which can be difficult to resist. Whilst it can produce gems, it can also waste a lot of time.

Managers may well have to impose restrictions on staff access for fear of time-wasting through sheer curiosity or addictiveness. As software can sit on your PC at home to censor out unsuitable material for the young, managers may well have to contemplate similar measures at work, such as limiting who has access, and who can do what.

Managing People

The convergence of telecommunications and computing which has made the Internet possible offers us flexibility in our working lives on a scale hitherto unimagined.

By exploiting the Internet and other communications technologies such as video-conferencing and computer integrated telephony, colleagues, partners, buyers and sellers no longer have to sit by side, nor even travel, to meet to conduct their business. The benefits of remote working include:

- Work requiring concentration can be done in isolation
- There are savings to be made on travelling time and costs, with knock-on environmental benefits
- Employees can enjoy greater flexibility and employers incur lower 'office' costs through space savings
- Teamworking is enabled between people in different locations. One of the ways of working towards this is by using an Intranet. This enables information-sharing using the same software, network technology and computer language as the Internet. Intranets exist only within organisations, secure from the outside. People on the inside can see and share information and look out to the Internet, but outsiders cannot get in
- People unable to take up normal 'office hours' can be recruited
- As the Internet operates across time and space, there need be no more 'normal' office hours

There are implications for managers, however:

- Management may fear a loss of control with an 'invisible' workforce
- A sense of loyalty, cohesion, even understanding may be difficult to maintain with a dispersed workforce
- Remote working can lead to a sense of isolation and demotivation
- People may resent the loss of their own space and work 'status'

- The social side of work – along with those accompanying social skills – may disappear
- The facilitation of personal networking can lead to leaking of sensitive information as well as time-wasting
- Information sharing makes it easier for employees to make their own judgements, to challenge authority and threaten the power-base of the organisation

The impact on organisations and individuals may be considerable. One implication is that short- or fixed-term contracts, already on the increase, will become the norm as people sell their skills to fit organisational and personal needs.

For further exploration of this, and other aspects of virtual working, see *Understanding the Virtual Organisation* in this series.

Managing Information

Intellectual property and copyright

As soon as any intellectual property – documents or images, graphs or text – is available through the Internet, then it (currently) has no monetary value as most information is available free to all. This is changing with new controls emerging to turn surfers into potential customers or subscribers. But the problem goes deeper than that. If, in due course, a customer pays for a document on the Internet, and receives that document via the Internet, copyright law exists to stop him or her changing its appearance and retransmitting it, either free or for a fee to thousands of others, for example, on the open newsgroups. But copyright law is hard enough to police and enforce in the real world; on the Internet it becomes virtually impossible.

Some have said that the Internet will bring about a massive change to copyright legislation, others that copyright itself will influence the character of business on the Internet.

Although copyright can be horrendously complex, there are fundamentally two things to remember:

(i) documents you, or your organisation, have produced are yours to dispose of in any appropriate legal manner you wish
(ii) documents, or pictures, or designs – intellectual property – produced by others are not available for you to re-copy, or retransmit without permission, payment or a licence.

It is increasingly accepted that technological developments have now far outstripped the capacity of current copyright legislation to control the passage of intellectual property. This issue is currently stretching the legislative bodies of the US Senate and the EU. The focus of copyright is also shifting towards the act of transmitting a document as opposed to just copying it. In the meantime be wary of making your valuable documentation available over the net; it could rapidly lose any commercial value you attach to it.

It is not yet certain what the outcome of this will be, although one possibility is that it might well lead to experimentation with imaginative pricing policies.

When an item consists of intellectual property that can be delivered to the customer via the Internet, ease of reproduction and retransmission may initiate lower pricing for that item in order to reduce the incentive for piracy. The Internet's very character could, as business takes hold, make things cheaper than they have been through traditional means.

Security and Control

Because intellectual property is key to competitive advantage, ensuring that your information is secure has become a major concern on the Internet. If you are exchanging information for payment over the Internet for payment, you will need to make sure that the transaction is private and confidential and that you are selling to someone who is who they say they are.

The information industry has been looking at encryption and firewalls for some years in order to be able to protect private, sensitive or valuable documents and guarantee their safe transmission. Firewalls are secure electronic devices which prevent unauthorised access. Encryption is the term used for scrambling messages so that only the intended recipient – with the appropriate software – can read them. Both firewalls and encryption have implications for secure financial operations on the Internet.

Managing Finance

Most early experiences of attempts to generate revenue on the Internet have been speculative at best. Success stories have been few and far between, largely because of lack of confidence in the security mechanisms, irrespective of whether they work or not, and the very 'newness' and 'difference' of the Internet as a shopping medium. For these reasons it is better to view your Internet operation as a cost centre – at least in the short-term – and an investment for the future, rather than as a profit centre.

Paying over the Web

The mid-1990s have witnessed many electronic payment pilot schemes with major banks collaborating with software companies to trial secure payment mechanisms. Some systems have involved securing online credit card payments by channelling card numbers direct to a firewalled computer so that they are not accessible to other parties from the Internet. In other initiatives, retailers and banks have used a common standard of encryption called SSL to transmit financial data. Those working on the systems say that it would take a powerful computer a year to crack each encrypted message. SSL is estimated to offer as much security as a telephone or mail order transaction.

Similarly, MasterCard and Visa have collaborated on software which scrambles credit card numbers into a code which is then transmitted to the seller. Secure Electronic Transaction (SET) offers virtually uncrackable encryption and will require both sender and recipient to have software supplied by the card issuer to prove to each other who they are. In due course passwords and bank cards will be replaced by smartcards with their own programmable chip allowing purchases to be made from anywhere, not just your own computer.

Alternative investigations include opening an account for small and anonymous purchases with 'e-cash'. There are several versions including DigiCash and CyberCash. Customers open an account with an 'e-bank', store their 'e-cash' on a card or in the bank's computer, and use a password to authorise payment for goods. Another version of e-cash is NatWest's Mondex, tested in the mid 1990s and now majority-owned by MasterCard.

In 1997 the Royal Bank of Scotland piloted payment of bills, money transfer and viewing of account details 24 hours a day, seven days a week on the Internet; Tesco offered Internet access to, and selection from, 20,000 product lines; the Online Bookshop in Oxford offered a share flotation over the Internet and doubled its value; and Microsoft was at the forefront of developments to collaborate on common standards to amalgamate these disparate initiatives. In the USA a group of leading banks was collaborating with IBM to build an integrated PC/Internet banking platform.

One forecast estimates that 80 per cent of European banks will provide a full Internet banking service by the year 2000. He would be brave who would argue that they will not succeed – even if they might be a bit late!

Technically, many of the payment and security mechanisms reported earlier today are as sound and secure as any other means of payment. The single reporting of one successful hacker, however, is still enough to destroy the fragile confidence that credit card numbers are safe online.

Taxation

Huge amounts of tax revenues are being lost as electronic forms of trading begin to evolve. The US Treasury estimates that $3 billion have been lost in tax revenue as consumers make purchases over the Internet from mail order companies.

As some initiatives explore the possibility of micro-billing – enabling the billing of low-value products by levying payments on the quantity of data transmitted, however small – a European Union working party has examined a 'bit tax' under which each electronic transmission – fax, telephone call, Internet session – could be logged and taxed. This would mean a shift away from value-added tax to one based on the quantity of information sent or received. Proposals are exploratory as commentators point to 'unfairness': taxation does not seem fair where zero value is gained. On the other hand, if revenue is lost because the nature of the game is changing, then the taxman will pursue those revenues by means which are more in line with the emerging information society.

Making Money on the Internet

In Europe, success stories are more isolated than in the US, although predictions forecast a Web market worth £30 billion by the year 2005. While impossible to substantiate at present, current growth and progress make it hard to dismiss the trend, if not the accuracy, of the projection. If progress is currently faster in the USA than in Europe, it is probably because of a more mature and unified market which is more attuned to electronic traffic, and the greater unification in culture, language and currency.

A glance at the US market, however, reveals that companies are not so much selling to domestic consumers as to other companies on the Internet. The business to business market is thought to have developed faster than consumer retailing because online shopping has to compete with the mix of requirements that the real thing affords: providing the right product at the best price on the one hand, and social interaction on the other. Perhaps the main reason for the progress of the business market is that industrial consumers can settle their bills by monthly accounts instead of by credit card on a one-off basis.

Developing an Internet Strategy

The 1990s has witnessed a rush by many organisations to be 'up on the Net'. Hundreds of thousands of organisations have established Web sites, not necessarily for sound strategic reasons, but rather for fear of missing out, for believing unprovable assertions that they will be out of business if they don't, or for hoping that there really might have been a free and easy market in cyberspace, ready to exploit. The reality in many cases has not lived up to the dream – numbers of site visits do not translate readily into cash transactions.

In reaction to this, organisations are now attempting to get to grips with what the Internet really offers as a communications medium and are trying to integrate their planning for the Internet into their business strategy.

In this second phase of Internet adoption, organisations are beginning to look at:

- Specific market sectors and the population likely to use the Internet for business purposes
- Structuring their information retrieval capability to specific business purposes such as supplier and customer communications, and market and distribution channels
- Using the Internet to support the organisation's key business activities such as providing the first port of call for product and distribution information

It is now becoming important to determine both the level and pace of Internet adoption and to determine resource allocation for Internet operations by asking about:

- *The value of information on the Internet*
  How many gems – as opposed to how much dross – are really out there? To find this out will require regular monitoring of the Internet.
- *Cultural fit with the Internet*
  How 'Internet-friendly' is the organisation's staff? If there is value to be had, do we have the right approach and the best staff and training to profit from it? How much do we need to change?
- *The Internet market*
  Is the profile of our best – or most likely – customer among the profiles of the growing numbers of Internet users?
- *Product/service suitability*
  Not all products or services may be suitable for the Internet. Information-based services may well have an advantage over manufacturing. Close awareness of customer needs is again the key.
- *Your customers*
  Is your existing customer-base likely to switch to Internet trading, or not? If not, Internet operations means tackling not only a new medium, but also new markets.

- *Internet functions*
  How do the Web, email, newsgroups and FTP relate to the business activities of R&D, recruitment, buying and selling, marketing and after-sales service? Look back at the map on p 49, there is more to the Internet than just the Web.
- *Policies which address:*
  - ethical questions of ownership and access to information. How might the power-base of the organisation change if information is to be available to all?
  - what information should be imported from and exported to the Internet. How and when is information revised and updated? Are there policies in place to guide employees on what they can use the Internet for? Who is accountable for what is up there and what is not?

The strategy should identify the opportunities and benefits of the Internet, tackle organisational and implementation issues and be – in itself – changing and developing to reflect the nature of the medium.

Conclusion

The Internet has made, and will continue to make, enormous inroads into our personal and working lives. Today we have indicated some areas of consideration for the immediate future and raised questions the answers to which will have a determining influence on the progress of the Internet.

How soon will it be before:

- Most large companies aggressively encourage telecommuting?
- Access to remote computers is commonplace in the home?
- Pricing strategies for communications are modified?
- Standards for security and secure payment generate confidence for widespread usage?
- Hacking and viruses pose less of a threat?
- A government policy emerges?
- Better quality information outweighs dross on the Internet?
- Business can be guaranteed the levels of performance to run the virtual business?
- The high-speed, high-performance and high-capacity telecommunications cables – the much hyped broadband cables capable of piping 500 channels to the home – are installed?

Some of these questions will be answered sooner rather than later. In the meantime it is important to be aware of the issues for you and your business, and, if you haven't yet, to take some action.

The organisation, however large or small, public or private, profit-making or charitable, manufacturing or service, needs to know how rapidly the Internet is changing to cater for business needs and the major issues to consider when becoming connected. It will need to establish strategies and tactics on the Internet; it will need to know which major operations need to be performed and the best way of performing them; and it will need to know how to resource them and assimilate a different scale of costs and new cost structures. Most importantly it will need to adopt a new vision, or way of looking at how the business can work without the traditional constraints of time, space or physical resources.

As a final word, put the Internet to use; many have found it rewarding and useful.

- Establish an effective connection to the Internet and promote its use within the organisation
- Start to use email and sign up with one or two specialist discussion groups
- Make time to explore the resources relevant to your own and the organisation's needs
- Become familiar with the Internet so that it becomes an integrated part of your day
- Plan to start doing business on the Internet